HELP! MY DOG DOESN'T LIKE BEING LEFT ALONE

The proactive approach to help your lonely dog

Tim Jackson

Copyright © 2020 by Tim Jackson

All rights reserved. No part of this publication may be reproduced, distributed, or transmitted in any form or by any means, including photocopying, recording, or other electronic or mechanical methods, without the prior written permission of the author, except in the case of brief quotations embodied in critical reviews and certain other noncommercial uses permitted by copyright law.

Published by WriterMotive
www.writermotive.com

Contents

Praise for Our Training and Behaviour Programmes 5

Introduction 9

Chapter One: Why dogs do not like being left alone 15

Chapter Two: Is your dog showing signs that he does not like being left alone? 22

Chapter Three: Building up confidence and independence 30

Chapter Four: You are what you eat 39

Chapter Five: Teaching your dog to settle 43

Chapter Six: Identifying the triggers 48

Chapter Seven: Changing the place where you leave your dog 56

Chapter Eight: Gradual Departures 60

Chapter Nine: The dos and the don'ts 64

Chapter Ten: Your goal to success 72

Bonuses 75

About the Author 78

Other Books by the Author 80

Acknowledgements 81

Praise for Our Training and Behaviour Programmes

What Some of Our Clients Have to Say About Our Training and Behaviour Programmes

"Our three-year-old west highland terrier wasn't responding well to our new shih tzu puppy. We'd expected jealousy etc., but he was really fearful and became aggressive, withdrawn and generally seemed depressed. He'd stopped playing with us, and we were getting to the point of returning our puppy.

Tim came out and spent some time with us and our westie... of course, it was us that got the training lol! Tim was brilliant, gave an honest assessment of our situation and changes we could make immediately as well as training exercises we could do with the dogs.

After perseverance and practice, we now have two happy dogs and the confidence to continue with the work. I can definitely recommend Tim. Thanks so much for a happier life."
Vicki Kenyon

"I have a one-year-old Red Cocker and was having a lot of problems with his behaviour – my fault as I totally spoilt him from day one. Tim was recommended by my dog groomer. I rang and booked a telephone consultation. I felt at ease as soon as I spoke to him. He was so lovely and made me feel positive from the start.

We got out of the programme everything we needed. It's up to us now to keep putting in the work we learnt.

After the first lesson, we saw a huge improvement in our dog's behaviour. I would definitely recommend Tim and Pets2impress."
Sara White

"We bought two puppies and found it extremely difficult to do anything with them; we needed help.

We got with Tim at Pets2impress, who came and did an assessment. He informed us that they had fear-based aggression towards other dogs, and he put our minds at ease, knowing that there was something we could do to help them.

Without Tim's help, I could not have coped. I can't recommend Pets2impress enough."
Mr and Mrs Selby

Help! My Dog Doesn't Like Being Left Alone

"My partner and I adopted a dog from Europe. All was well until three months later when he started to show signs of aggression towards other dogs and men.
We contacted Tim for an assessment and booked him for training. We did everything Tim suggested, and now our dog can be around other dogs (even daycare) and people. We now have learnt the tools and techniques needed to recognise when our dog is in a situation he is not comfortable with and are able to use the training commands to get him out of it which means no more aggression! Thank you Tim."
Mr S Scott

"I have a male dog called Storm, who is a Newfoundland cross bullmastiff and has an anxiety issue. He got to the point where he is very fearful of strangers and would growl and bark to scare them off. After several weeks training with Tim and him bringing various people along to the house, Storm has now started to relax and is nowhere near as bad as he was. I will continue to use pets2impress with Storm as I can't believe the results they are having with Storm. I am over the moon, and I can now actually start to relax. If you're thinking of using these guys then it's money well spent."
Lee Brown

"I have absolutely loved taking part in the online course. I love my time spent with Paddy teaching him new tricks etc., and this course has opened up a whole new load of ideas that I can use and implement on our day to day activity that didn't even cross my mind. I thought it was going to be a real struggle for him during this isolation period with the lack of exercise and stimulation that he is used to on a daily basis. He is used to a good 2/3 walks per day as well as 2 – 3 full days at Pets2impress daycare, so naturally, I thought he would be bored during lockdown and bouncing off the walls with energy. During this course, his tail has never stopped wagging, and I've found that he is just as tired at night during this time as he was after a busy day on the go day. Thank you, Tim, for everything you have done."
Samantha Heley

"Having the resources from Tim at Pets2impress available through the lockdown has been invaluable. The changes and help provided have kept our puppy active, stimulated and happy! In a massive change to normal routine, my worry was that Cobie would suffer and lose her confidence that she had gained, but instead, she has learnt so much, and we have the knowledge to keep things going after this is over."
Amy McFalus

"My Black Labrador Charlie had an amazing time completing the online challenges in the Pets2Impress 14-day challenge, he learnt a lot, and so did I. It was both fun and educational! I ordered him the isolation pack so he could get some toys and treats as a reward for his hard work. The pack gave me some more ideas on how to challenge him and train him too."
Anni Jowett

"I would just like to say that Tim came to Stockton on tees yesterday to see my Mam with her dog Mavis Tim has made my Mam feel that she can help Mavis and my Mam isn't upset anymore now she knows what she needs to do to help her I'm so thankful for your help highly recommend this company thank you so so much."
Victoria Ainsley

Introduction

At the time of writing this book, the world is currently experiencing one of the scariest medical emergencies seen in the last 100 years.

The Coronavirus has thrown our world as we know it upside down; we are all worried and scared about what the future has to bring.

When the outbreak first hit one of my biggest concerns, apart from the welfare of my friends and family was the effects this would have on our dogs.

The world is currently in lockdown and routines have been thrown out of the window not just for us but for our dogs as well, and naturally, this is going to have a huge impact on their lives and wellbeing.

Being at home all day and every day with our dogs is not what they are used to, and a lot of dogs are naturally going to struggle when things get back to normal... whatever that normal may look like.

Although I write this book during this time, this is not where I want to start. I want to take you back to the year 2006, the year when I bought my first puppy, the lovely and adorable Lady.

Lady was a German Shepherd who I had the pleasure of spending the next 12 years with, I bought her from a back street breeder (mistake one) and to top that off I bought her for my girlfriend at the time (mistake two), and I got her when she was only five weeks old (mistake three).

I already had an elderly dog at home, but my girlfriend at the time had her heart set on a German Shepard. I was a young (may I add handsome) 20-year-old with very little experience with dogs.

I was currently working at a veterinary practice as an auxiliary nurse getting ready to start my training to become a veterinary nurse. My knowledge of dogs at this time was very little, and I certainly had no clue about training or behaviour. Some would say I should have done my homework before getting a dog and trust me 14 years on I would agree! I am sure I am not the only owner who bought a puppy on impulse and went for the cute factor, and I certainly won't be the last!

I had taken two weeks annual leave when I got her so that I could be with her as naturally it is a very scary time for any puppy leaving their Mam and siblings and I wanted to socialise her to the world and work on her training.

This is where it all went wrong because the second Lady was officially mine; she was treated like a little princess. On her first night in her new home, she snuggled in the bed with me, I took her everywhere with me and never left her side.

She was an adorable little ball of fluff what was not to resist… she was certainly the best girl that had stepped into my life. It is difficult to not want to be with your puppy in some cases people have waited a long time for the right puppy to come along or in my case I seen an advert my girlfriend at the time said she wanted a German Shepherd and because I was head over heels in love (or so I thought) I jumped at the chance.

Now I am naturally an outdoors person, and I like to keep busy, so wherever I went, Lady went too. Obviously, she couldn't go out for walks at this stage, so she was carried everywhere which worked well for the first few weeks, but she was a German Shepherd… she got big fast! I at least did something right, and that was socialising her to the world, I took her on public transport, I took her to my friends and family's homes and got her socialised with my friend's dogs who were fully vaccinated.

Once my two weeks annual leave were up, it was time to return to work and luckily at that time the girlfriend and I were still together, so she took Lady during the day and then brought her back to my house on a night time.

On days my girlfriend was at work I used to take her to work with me so young Mr Jackson had what he thought to be a perfect plan to ensure Lady was never left alone.

Now, as I am sure we are all aware, life never really goes to plan does it and not much long later the girlfriend and I split up… her loss, I guess!

Who got left with the dog? That's right…good old Mr Jackson. Don't get me wrong Lady was the best thing to have come from that relationship, and I wouldn't have changed her for the world.

Now back then there was no such thing as dog walkers that come in once a day and take your dog for a walk or lovely daycares that you can take your dog to whilst you are at work so they can socialise with other dogs and be cared for during the day and my boss then informed me that I couldn't bring Lady into work anymore as she was getting too big and they needed the kennel space for dogs that came in for emergencies and operations…rightly so.

Now I was stuck! I worked 10-hour shifts that were way too long to leave a dog for; the RSPCA recommend 4 hours maximum at any one time. Panic set in and I did not know what I was going to do, but at this stage, it still did not cross my mind that Lady may have developed separation anxiety as a result of not being left alone. To repeat, I was a young inexperienced dog owner who thought he was doing right by his newest addition.

I only had one option, and that was to rely on friends and family. Luckily, I lived just around the corner from my Mam so she was able to pop in and see to her so again I had a new plan of action, a plan I was fairly confident would work. I planned to walk Lady before and after work and then get my Mam to visit her during the day and spend some time with her.

Guess what? That plan never worked because Lady did not like being left alone (shocker), why would she, she had never been left alone before and boy did she rebel!

When I visit people's homes and do assessments on their dog, I have a scale in my head that goes from mild separation anxiety to major separation anxiety and certain boxes that I tick to assess the dog's behaviour when left alone.

Lady was off the scale! When she was left alone she would toilet (wees and poops), she would roll in it, spread it all over the floor. She would bark (annoying my neighbours – more on that later), howl and whine. She also bit a German Shephard shaped hole in the wall once in my rented accommodation…that was a fun day! Lady hated being alone and even hated it when I was asleep and not giving her any attention… one night she even attempted to poop on my face! Thankfully I am a light sleeper and woke up just at the right time. There are certain things you do not want your dog to do, and at this stage, Lady was ticking all of those boxes.

Life got very complicated very quickly, not only had I had my heart properly broken for the first time (get out those violins), but now I had this to deal with as well. Let's just say I wasn't very calm, but they do say when you go through a break-up distraction is the best thing and boy did Lady provide me with a distraction.

I was lost and unsure what to do, my experience then was certainly not what it is now, and I didn't have the first clue on what I should be doing to help Lady. I broke all of the rules which I will tell you about throughout this book, and I found myself dreading coming home to see what carnage she had done during my absence.

Leaving home then became a worry because I didn't want to leave her and I could guarantee every night, I came home Moody Margaret from upstairs would complain to me. In all fairness, she did have warrant to complain, but it was not what I needed at that time, and it just added to my stress levels even more.

I had a decision to make 1. I leave my job and stay at home every day with Lady 2. I rehome Lady or 3. I do something about it!

Naturally, I couldn't leave my job, I loved my job and was just about to start my training, and although I thought about it a number of times, I couldn't give her up, I loved her too much despite the stress and frustration.

So what did I do? How did I correct this unwanted behaviour and ensure Lady was calm and relaxed when being home alone?

The answer is simple, I put in the work, and I worked extremely hard with her because I never got a dog to give up on her. Was it easy? No of course not because sadly nothing ever is but am I glad I put in the work? Absolutely!

Lady went on to live until the age of 12 years old, and she was an absolutely adorable dog with such a kind and gentle nature. Had I not put in the work and rehomed her, god knows what would have happened to her, would someone else have been as patient? Would someone else have given up on her and then rehomed her again? These were all of the questions that went through my head when I did initially think about rehoming her, and I am sure you too have thought the same thing.

This book was created to try and help people who have a dog that suffers from separation anxiety as I know what it is like to feel so low and frustrated but yet also wanting to do the right thing for your dog. Sadly, so many dogs end up in shelter as a result of unwanted behaviour, and I hope this book will prevent that from happening. This book was designed for anyone that has a dog scared to be left alone and for those that feel they have tried everything else.

I was so close to giving up on Lady, and I do not want anyone else to have to feel like that so within this book you will learn step by step what you need to do to help your scared to be home alone pooch.

I do not believe in, spray collars, shock collars or any form of negative based methods of training, so if that is what you are looking for, I suggest you look elsewhere. A scared dog is already in a negative situation, by using negative based methods of training you will add further negative associations, and you will never correct the problem; in fact, there is a good chance it will make the problem worse.

Before we can look at correcting this issue, we need to have a look and understand why are dogs feeling like this.

Chapter One

Why dogs do not like being left alone

Dogs are naturally very sociable animals, and they naturally would live within a family group. Over thousands of years, they have evolved to live alongside humans, to work with us or to be companions.

Some dogs would happily spend every minute of every day in our company whereas some dogs are happy to spend time with their own kind.

There are an estimated 10 million dogs in the UK, and an estimated 1.8 million dogs reported to be suffering from separation anxiety. This, as I am sure you will agree, is a huge number and brings a huge problem for a lot of dog owners.

All dogs, as I am sure you will agree, are unique in their own little way, they all have their own traits and characters. Whilst some breeds are more prone to separation anxiety some can develop it over time, but one thing is for sure being alone just doesn't come naturally to a lot of dogs which is why so many dogs struggle being left alone.

Nowadays people work a lot of hours, and 9-5 jobs are now a distant memory. As people are out of the house more in a lot of cases, that means the dogs are left for longer periods of time.

Bearing in mind, the RSPCA recommends a dog be left for a maximum of 4 hours at any one time, in a lot of cases dogs are left for 6 hours plus and for an animal as sociable as a dog this by any means was way too long.

During the outbreak of the COVID-19 restrictions were put in place, and people were told to stay and home and only leave home if it was essential. I am sure you will agree there was only so much you could watch on the television, only so much cleaning that you could do before your day started to drag.

Help! My Dog Doesn't Like Being Left Alone

I guess with modern technology we are lucky; we have access to the internet, televisions, we can read a book or play on the X-box. We have things to keep our minds occupied throughout the day. I cannot imagine how boring life must have been in 1918 when the outbreak of influenza occurred. Dogs do not get that luxury, when a dog is stuck at home alone what do they have to keep themselves occupied?

Is it any wonder they do not like being left home alone?

Give me 1 hour stuck in a room alone with nothing to do, I think I would protest too!

I think we all know far too well now how boring life can be stuck indoors all day long, which is why I get so surprised at how long people leave their dogs for on a daily basis. Do not get me wrong, I totally understand people need to work to make a living however these days we are blessed with the fact there are dog walkers, there are daycares available that you can take your dog to during the day.

But what causes separation anxiety? 9/10 times it is a learnt behaviour; the dog learns very quickly he does not like being left home alone.

When you first bring your puppy home, you love nothing more than spending time with him, working on his toilet training, doing some training with him, playing with his toys, snuggling up on the sofa on a night time. We have all been there because it is a natural instinct we have to want to love and care for our newest family member, but one of the most important lessons I would say most fail to teach is how to help your dog cope being left alone.

That was certainly something I did wrong with Lady, she came everywhere with me, and she was never left alone because I didn't like the thought of leaving her alone. Although that may have seemed like the best thing at the time, in the long run, I was causing myself some major problems and causing Lady a lot of unnecessary stress.

Lady became very reliant on me and naturally enjoyed my company – I provided her with everything she needed. When I look back, it was no wonder she got so upset being left by herself because I had never taught her how to be by herself. Before I got her, she had spent five weeks with her Mam and littermates and then she came to me and for her first few months with me she was never left alone, albeit it, she wasn't with me 100% of the time she still had some form of human contact at all times throughout the day.

I don't think many people like being left alone, yes, it's nice from time to time but a lot of people like to be in a relationship or if they are home alone, they may phone a friend or go out to the pub or out for a meal. We have that luxury to do what we want when we want (in reason of course), dogs, however, do not have that luxury when they are home alone, they are home alone, and that's it!

Separation anxiety is a very horrible behaviour to live with not just for you but ultimately for your dog. It causes dogs to panic at the idea of being left home alone. That panic may be so overwhelming for them that when you leave, they become destructive, they bark or howl, they pace, they salivate, or they demonstrate housebreaking issues.

What we have to remember is your dog does not understand that you need to pop to the shops, you need to go to work or your out on a romantic date. Your dog doesn't know when or even if you're coming back. In most circumstances, you are your dog's whole world, and if you begin to look at things from your dog's point of view, it is no wonder some dogs have such a difficult time being left alone.

As owners, we can also make those feelings worse for our dogs, and I'm going to share with you what I did with Lady, which I will say now was all wrong!

My normal day to day would consist of getting up, walk Lady, shower, dressed, breakfast and then dash out of the house to catch the number 7 bus.

Once Lady had her walk, she followed me around the house wherever I went, and she watched my every move. At this point, she was pacing and panting a lot. I would often trip over her as I tried to move from room to room. During my mad rush, I even lost my temper with her for getting under my feet.

Just as I was about to leave, she was making a mad dash for the front door to try and leave with me to which I had to quickly pick her up (not easy picking up a huge German Shephard may I just add) and put her in the kitchen. I quickly said, "Be good Lady, won't be long" (I said this every time that I left her as I went to work or went to the shops etc.). I had a strange house, the kitchen was in the basement, and that's where she was left, but every day as I ran up the stairs I could see her peering through the baby gate looking at me run away– talk about making you feel guilty.

I then took myself to work. During the day she had a visit from my Mam, and I can all but guarantee every time my Mam visited, I received a text message to inform me of the mess Lady had caused.

That immediately had me worried, stressed and also frustrated if I am completely honest with you because I knew that despite my lovely Mam cleaning up after my dog that same mess would be there when I returned as once my Mam had left Lady again would experience this terrifying feeling of being left alone.

I had hoped this would get better with age (I could kick myself now), but in fact, it got worse as she got older and the more times I left her, the worse it seemed to get.

Now let me tell you what happened when I returned home from work. I went straight down to see her, and without fail all of the kitchen cupboards had been emptied, she had toileted all over the kitchen floor and then trailed in it and being a long-haired German Shepherd I am sure you can imagine the mess she caused.

I had an island in the middle of the kitchen with wooden bar stools, each day there was less and less of the legs as she had clearly been chewing her way through them bit by bit.

My first reaction when I saw what she had done was to say "who's done that?" or "you bad girl" to which she would give me that guilty look – the look where she turns her head and looks at me from the corner of her eye.

I am sure at some point we have all seen that look, and to me, at that moment in time I thought to myself, she knows what she has done – I'll tell you soon how she didn't have a clue why she was being told off.

Normally after being home and just as I had started to tackle the destruction Lady had left, I would receive a knock on the door from Moody Margaret from upstairs who would always knock to tell me Lady had been barking constantly all day long.

Now there was no such thing as doggy cameras back then so I could not check in on Lady during the day on my smartphone so I had to take Moody Margaret's word for it. However, there was one day when Lady had been in work with me as she was not feeling very well so the house had been empty all day and when I returned home I got a knock on the door to say she had been barking all day. Interesting, I said considering she was with me all day.

That put Moody Margaret in her place and chances are she was exaggerating how much Lady had been barking, as I suspect most neighbours do. I still feel she was in her right to complain to me because there is nothing worse than having to listen to the neighbour's dog barking throughout the day.

By this time, I was stressed and more frustrated that Lady would do this, was she punishing me for going to work? For leaving her?

Once the house was back to normal, off we went for a walk, and by the time I sat down for my tea, it was rather late and then off to bed I would go to follow the same routine the next day.

Owning a dog was not working out how I had imagined it to be. I had friends who had dogs, and their dogs appeared to be the perfect example of how a dog should be so naturally I thought I was being punished for something I must have done in a previous life.

Now, where did I go wrong? Firstly, I never recognised that Lady was, in fact, stressed before I had even left the house. Secondly, I had to pretty much wrestle her to the kitchen. Thirdly I always said "be good Lady, I won't be long" which I will explain more later in the book why that was a bad thing, and then on my return, I told her off for the mess she had created during my absence.

That is where most people go wrong. They tell their dogs off on their return for something they did 3 hours ago. Now believe it or not but dogs cannot build an association with what you are telling them off for that they did hours ago the reason they give you that guilty look is because of the way you are reacting.

The guilty look is actually a calming signal because the dog is frightened of the behaviours you are displaying, the raised voice, that pointed finger. If you display aggressive behaviours either vocally or physically (may I just point out neither are the correct methods) then your dog will respond to the behaviours you are displaying not think "oops, really shouldn't have pooped all over the floor, now I'm in a lot of trouble".

When a dog is feeling frightened or anxious, they will toilet, it is an involuntary action, but it makes them feel a bit better, even if just for a short period of time. The next time you watch a horror and you get a shock go to the toilet, I can guarantee you will feel slightly less scared. Over time the dog learns that this motion of going to the toilet makes them feel ever so slightly better, which is why they repeat it.

Now another issue I also had was by coming home and telling Lady off, I was adding to her stress because now not only was she stressed and anxious that I wasn't there she was also stressed at the thought of me coming back because of how I was going to react. She learnt through experience that when I returned home, I wasn't going to give her the greeting she expected; instead, I was going to shout at her. Trust me when I got told this from the behaviourist that came to see me at the time, I felt pretty guilty myself because I could build that association unlike Lady and all the other dogs out there.

Knowing this now, it breaks my heart that I ever put Lady in that situation. However, I honestly thought at the time that was the best way to deal with the situation but because I now know what I know about dogs, I wish someone had come and told me off for being such a plonker.

So now we can hopefully understand why dogs do not like being left alone, and maybe you can relate to my story with Lady and if you have been experiencing similar things with your dog and have maybe reacted in a similar stressed and frustrated manner to the way I did try not to beat yourself up.

I spent a long time regretting the decisions I made with Lady from day one, but in the end, I realised I could not change what has already been done, but I can change how things are done in the future, and that's what I did, and boy was it worth it. Just think about the message in from the classic Disney film, The Lion King when that crazy monkey hits Simba over the head and says "it's in the past, it doesn't matter" followed by Simba who says "yeah but it still hurts". The crazy monkey was right, you can either run from your mistakes or learn from them… see watching Disney films growing up did teach me something after all.

I will be sharing those secrets with you very soon but before that let's have a look at some common behaviours a dog may display to suggest they have separation anxiety.

Chapter Two

Is your dog showing signs that he does not like being left alone?

A dog that is suffering from separation anxiety may display a number of behaviours, some (like Lady) may display quite a few whilst others may be a little bit more subtle and others you may not even be aware that your dog does struggle being left alone. Just because they do not show any signs does not mean that they are happy being left alone.

I would always advise a full examination from your veterinary surgeon to begin with to make sure your dog is fit and well in himself and to rule out any medical concerns. There may be a medical issue that is making your dog toilet so much when left alone. In fact, it may turn out your dog doesn't have separation anxiety after all.

Separation anxiety is triggered when dogs become upset because they are separated from their humans. Some dogs will even show signs of stress prior to the owner leave, and some will try to prevent the owner from leaving, as Lady did when she ran towards the door just as I was about to leave.

Almost immediately after the owner leaves, the dog will start to display distress behaviours, one of the more common behaviours is barking, and this is the dog's way of shouting saying 'wait, you have forgotten about me, come back'. This natural instinct relates back to the descendant of the dog, wolves. When cubs leave the den for the first time with Mam and Dad, it is not uncommon for one, two or even all of the cups to wander off, the world is a big place with lots to explore and lots of new smells to investigate.

Eventually, the cub will realise, hang on a minute, where are Mam and Dad? The cub will then let out a cry and in some cases a howl to alert the rest of the pack where he/she is. The rest of the pack finds him/her, and then that behaviour gets reinforced, just like a dog's barking or howling behaviour gets reinforced because eventually, we return home.

This in itself can immediately cause stress for the owner as they know they have to leave the dog whether that be for work or to go to the shops. Due to this, there are some owners that always make sure the dog is never left because they can't bear to see their dog so distressed. This, of course, will never correct the problem but instead will make the problem worse.

By never leaving your dog alone, you are not building any confidence or independence for the dog; instead, you create a dog that is 100% reliant on their owner. Imagine if your partner took unwell and you had to take them to the hospital, what would you do with the dog then? It is good practice to work with your dog's confidence of being left alone just in case unknown situations arise. As much as I love my dogs I could never have imaged being trapped in my own home or only able to go to places I could take the dog with me, we all have lives to live as well.

I understand why you don't want to leave your dog, trust me I went through the same situation with Lady, but as proved when the time came where I had to leave her alone because I had no other option, boy did I learn my lesson.

Let's start by looking at why dogs can get distressed before their owners even leave.

Dogs are incredible creatures and far more intelligent than we give them credit for, and although they don't know what day of the week it is or what time it is, they certainly can pick up when you are about ready to leave.

We all have our own little routines when we get up in a morning and get ready for work, but there will be a number of things you do that your dog will pick up on. We call these trigger points.

To explain, I will talk you through my normal routine in a morning on a weekday as well as on a weekend.

In the morning, I get up, go to the toilet and brush my teeth. I then take the dog for a walk. On return, he gets his breakfast whilst I get a shower and get dressed for work. I then come downstairs to eat my breakfast, and then I empty the dishwasher and put on a load in the washing machine.

I then pack my bag, put on my coat and shoes and get my keys and then off to work I go. (I could be just like one of the seven dwarfs from Snow White, high ho, high ho, it's off to work I go)

On the weekend however I still get up, go to the toilet and brush my teeth. I then go downstairs and take the dog for his walk. So far, that part of the routine is the same. On return, I give him his breakfast, and then I get mine, but normally I sit down and watch a bit of TV with my son, and I may choose to lounge around a bit before going upstairs for a shower.

Naturally, when not at work I don't wear my uniform and once dressed, I will return downstairs and spend some time with the children. Morning routines on a weekend are a lot more chilled than say that of a weekday.

Although there are similarities to my day to day routine, my weekend routine is very different from my weekday routine, and dogs can pick up on that.

One of the biggest differences in my routine is on a weekend when I return from walking the dog I sit down and watch a bit of TV, as opposed to running around because I'm late.

When I get showered and come back downstairs, I am not in my work uniform and not so much in a rush to empty the dishwasher or put a load of washing on, instead, I spend some time with the children.

On a weekday there are certain trigger points that the dog could pick up on to suggest I am about to leave him, such as wearing my uniform, such as putting on my coat and shoes and looking for the car keys.

I am certainly not as chilled on a weekday as I am on the weekend and the dog will be able to pick up on those things.

The dog over time will be able to recognise certain things I do and the order of the things I do them, and that's what we call trigger points. The dog starts to recognise this order of events and associates them with me leaving the house without them.

When Lady was a puppy, she would follow me around as soon as I had breakfast and watch my every move and as I continued on with my normal routine, she got herself more and more wound up. She would pace, pant and on some days drool. Most days, she would also refuse to eat her breakfast as it was more important to her to know where I was and what I was doing.

When the time came to leave, she used to try and dart out with me or block the exit point, hence why I had to pick her up and put her in the kitchen.

Once I left, I could immediately hear her barking, and I would walk away feeling stressed and worried about her, and that continued until I knew my Mam was with her and then it started again once I knew my Mam had left.

There are a number of behaviours a dog suffering from separation anxiety can display, and over this chapter, I am going to discuss some of the more common behavioural concerns that owners bring to me that they experience with their dog.

Urinating and Defecating

A lot of people seem to think that the dog does this out of protest, I promise it is not out of protest… your dog may be clever, but he isn't that clever, and a dog's mind does not work like that.

Normally a dog will display these behaviours when he is feeling scared or anxious.

It is important to assess this issue as if your dog is toileting indoors when you are home. There is a good chance he just needs some work on his toilet training.

Barking and Howling

Dogs can bark for a number of different reasons, it is a way to express their emotions. This particular type of bark is like no other and very distinctive and will only be heard when the dog is left alone. Lady, being a German Shephard was very vocal, you only had to mention the W-word, and she would squeak away with excitement however the noise she made when left alone was clearly a noise from a dog that was very stressed, and if I am honest it was heartbreaking for me to listen too. I used to stand and listen at the door to see if she would settle, and some days she would, others I could still hear her as I went down the street. There were certain times I even went in to check on her and to try and calm her down, but of course, this resulted in making the problem worse.

Pacing

This is not the most obvious reported behavioural problem, and it tends to be those that have doggy cams that are able to pick up on it. Others may assume that the dog is actually ok when left alone when, in fact, he is not happy at all. Pacing basically involves the dog going backwards and forwards and not being able to settle.

Escaping

A dog suffering from separation anxiety may attempt to escape to get to his owner. He may attempt to dig or chew his way out of the area he is confined too. This can be very dangerous, and a lot of dogs can cause themselves an injury as a result. I will never forget a dog I worked with called George, who was an adorable but very nervous Shar-Pei. He had been crate trained from a puppy, and that was the place he was put in when left.

When I went and did an assessment on George's behaviour, we set up a live video feed to watch George when he was left alone. George was already distressed prior to the owner leaving, and when we were outside and were watching the live feed, he was digging and chewing at his crate. Previously, before I had visited, he had managed to chew and bend some of the bars of the crate and whilst watching the live feed he got his mouth caught in the bars, and the scream he made was unbearable. Naturally, we went straight back into the house, and when he was released, his mouth was bleeding from where he had attempted to chew his way out of the crate.

Coprophagia

Do not worry about the fancy word, it basically means the dog poops and then eats the poop. This is normally a sign to suggest that the dog is stressed however it is important to note if your dog is used to eating poop (I hope you are not eating during this chapter) when you are present then this doesn't necessarily mean he has separation anxiety. Thankfully, Lady never ate her own poop she just chose to roll in it instead, so I guess at least I could still get kisses.

Chewing, Digging and Destruction.

When left alone, some dogs will chew on objects such as table legs or door frames. Chewing is a way for the dog to relieve stress; however, in a lot of cases, this can lead to self-injury including broken teeth, cut nails or scraped paws.

If your dog chews and digs when you are present, then this one behaviour does not necessarily mean your dog has separation anxiety.

Not all dogs will display all of these behaviours; some may only show one or two, and some may be more subtle than others. Sadly for me (and maybe for you too) Lady displayed all of these behaviours which were not ideal in a rented accommodation.

There is no evidence to show exactly what causes separation anxiety, and there are potentially a lot of situations that can cause this behavioural problem. Some of the more common reasons are:

1. The dog has never been left alone before
2. Change of family, i.e. couple splits up
3. Change in routine
4. New home
5. Change in household members, i.e. sudden absence or the introduction of a baby.

We do of course need to rule out a number of potential reasons why your dog may be reacting the way he is when left alone as it could be that he doesn't have separation anxiety at all and the behaviours displayed could be for another reason.

Firstly, we need to rule out anything medical as in some situations house soiling can be caused by a urinary tract infection, hormone-related issues, age, diabetes, Cushing's disease etc. Also, if your dog is on regular medication at home check to see what the side effects are with those medications as in some cases, certain medicines can increase the need for the dog to toilet.

Help! My Dog Doesn't Like Being Left Alone

Depending on the age of your dog you also need to make sure he is fully house trained, plus if you are leaving him for 8 hours per day, there could also be the possibility that he just can't hold it in anymore. Imagine if you couldn't go to the toilet for a long period of time and you were desperate... it has to come out eventually right?

We also need to look at the potential that your dog is not just scent marking, especially common in males. If you think this may be the case, then maybe contact your veterinary practice and discuss the potential of getting him neutered as well as making sure you are putting in place necessary steps to prevent it. One of the easiest ways is to make sure all mess is cleaned up with non-biological washing powder or tonic water. These both have enzymes within them that help kill the ammonia within the urine whereas most household products actually have ammonia within the ingredients, which masks the scent your dog makes and then encourages them to go back to that same spot.

We have to expect that younger dogs sometimes engage in destructive behaviours which include chewing and digging as they explore their environment. This behaviour, though, could also be seen when the owners are home too.

Finally, we need to look at the potential that your dog could be bored, which is why he is being disruptive when left alone.

How long could you last in the house with no Wi-Fi, no mobile, no television, no book to read? I have to be honest, I would get bored fairly quickly, and sometimes dogs do too again, especially if they are being left for long periods of time throughout the day. As previously discussed dogs are naturally sociable animals and being left for long periods alone is not natural, is it any wonder they're bored? Chewing, digging, barking these can also be signs to say your housebound hound is just bored and looking for ways to entertain himself.

With regards to separation anxiety, you need to look at the full picture, i.e. how is your dog as you prepare to leave, what does he do as you leave, set up a doggy cam and watch what he does once you leave, what does he do when you return?

Certainly, it is frustrating when you have a dog that toilets indoors, that barks, that destroys things, but there are certain things you need to rule out first. Once you have ruled out the other potentials then it is the time to think separation anxiety.

Throughout this chapter we discussed the potential reasons separation anxiety may develop, we discussed some of the more common problems seen from dogs suffering from separation anxiety, and we looked at alternative reasons to why your dog could be displaying certain behaviours when left alone.

In the next chapter, we will be looking at the first steps to take to correct separation anxiety and to help build up some confidence for your dog when left alone.

Chapter Three

Building up confidence and independence

Some dogs hate being left by themselves, and as already mentioned, some will bark, howl or whine instinctively.

There are a number of steps you can take to help your dog feel less anxious when left alone, but to begin with, we need to look at increasing our dog's confidence and independence.

Firstly, we need to introduce a programme called 'Nothing in life is free', or in other words a learn to earn programme.

One of the nicest things you can do for your dog is to increase their confidence and independence and by implementing a 'Nothing in life is free' programme you will do just that.

Dog's love to learn and they love to work and by encouraging your dog to do that you automatically increase confidence and independence.

Now nothing in life is free doesn't mean we have to send them to work every day or get them to wash the car, pick up the shopping or crack on with the housework. It basically means if the dog wants something, he has to do something in order to get it.

Think of it this way, why do we go to work? Personally, I love work, but for most, it is to get paid at the end of the month. You have to put in that work to get what you want at the end.

As of now, your dog should work for everything so for example if he wants his dinner, have him sit or wait first, if he wants to go for a walk, get him to sit or if he wants to play with the new exciting toy you have just bought for him get him to lie down.

Personally, I do not mind what you get him to do, but he should do something in order for him to get something. Think of it like teaching a child to say please and thank you.

Everyone in the household needs to follow the same rules as this programme will not only make your dog more confident and more independent it will help to reduce anxiety.

We also need to put a stop to any attention-seeking behaviours and let me shout this loud and clear… I am not saying you cannot love your dog and I am certainly not saying you should not give your dog attention…what would be the point in having a dog?

We just need to make sure that all attention is invited by us and not the dog so, for example, imagine being sat on the settee on a night time watching television (I can't lie it would be Coronation Street for me!) and the dog comes and plonks one of his toys on you, waiting for you to throw it. This would be classed as attention on his terms; therefore, we should ignore these behaviours. You may find that the dog tries his hardest to get your attention, but it is very important that this is ignored.

There are three very important lessons to remember when it comes to ignoring your dog 1. Do not look, 2. Do not touch and 3. Do not speak – by breaking any of those rules you may as well out him on his back and give him a belly rub just for being cute.

If say after 30 minutes he gives up and starts to walk away and providing you want to, which I am sure you will, call him to you and give him lots of fuss and attention and by all means spend the rest of the evening playing with him, cuddling him, kissing him… whatever you like to do really.

So, by doing it this way, we can still give the dog attention, but now it is on our terms and not on the dogs.

It is not a case of trying to punish the dog as many would see it, in fact, it is the opposite we are implementing these steps to help build up confidence and independence, and we are teaching the dog, it's ok not to have attention from Mam or Dad every second of every day, I can quite happily entertain myself.

That is the first important change you must make moving forward. Now let us have a look at another very important aspect, a routine.

Dogs are creatures of habit, and they love to predict what is coming next, and we know the importance of a routine, we only need to think of how much our routines were thrown out the window during the COVID-19 Pandemic.

Dogs, like us, respond very well to routine and structure. Naturally, we want to keep things fun and exciting for the dogs too, so I always advise a varied routine, and I will explain what I mean by that now.

A routine for dogs should consist of five things and these are:

1. Feeding Times

Ideally, our dogs should be fed twice per day and at a similar time each day. Now I don't advise varying the diet, but I would advise varying the way you feed your dog.

Make feeding times fun and make your dog work for his meals. I very rarely use a food bowl for my dog, Buddy, instead I get him to work for his food, so this could involve placing his food in a Kong toy, a scatter feed in the garden, a homemade brain game or a puzzle game you can buy from the shops.

In fact, sometimes, I even use his daily allowance and do a training session with him.

We cannot forget food is a reward; therefore, he needs to work for it (Nothing in life is free) so ask him to 'sit' and 'wait' first before releasing him. By spicing up meal times, you encourage your dog to work for his food, and in the process, your dog is getting mentally stimulated, which is a guaranteed way to help reduce stress and anxiety.

One of Buddy's favourite games is to hand his Kong from the washing line. It takes him a long time to get the last bit of kibble, and he is always shattered afterwards… win-win.

Occasionally I place his daily allowance in a Kong toy, add a little bit of water to moisten up the biscuits, and then I freeze it overnight. The next day I hang it from the washing line and off he goes whilst I sit back with a cup of tea and watch him enjoy himself.

As with any form of mental stimulation, every 10 minutes equivalates to a 45 minute on lead walk so by the end of the day I have a very sleepy and calm dog, one of the reasons I knew the lockdown would not have an effect on him, especially with the earlier measures that were implemented of one bit of exercise per day. I should imagine a lot of owners struggled with that.

Now we can have a look at the second part of your dog's daily routine.

2. Walk Times

It goes without saying dogs need to be walked every day not just when the weather is fine! Walks are fun for your dog, and they give your dog the chance to make use of their natural senses, i.e. touch, smell, taste, sound and sight.

Walks give your dog a change of scenery, imagine being stuck indoors day in day out with no form of interaction... no doubt you would get bored pretty quickly which naturally would have an impact on your wellbeing, the same applies for dogs.

Dogs do not have the luxury of popping out when they like. They rely on us as owners to take them out. Walks shouldn't just involve heading to the field to throw a ball you should be making every walk into an adventure – certainly something we do at Pets2impress with the daycare dogs.

How to make a 1 hour walk seem like a 4 hour walk for your dog

Every walk should be an adventure, and you should use this time to really bond with your dog. On walks you should be giving your dog the chance to perform some natural agility, i.e. getting them to jump over fallen down trees, balancing, weaving in between trees, jumping over things etc.

You should also give your dog the chance to make use of his incredible sense of smell and if he wants to sniff every blade of grass then let him as scent work is a great way to help increase the dog's awareness and alertness and it will help to sharpen your dog's mind. Any form of scent work will also help increase your dog's self-esteem, which is very important for nervous or anxious dogs. Scent work is great for all dogs but in particular working, active and high energy breeds.

In June 2020, we were the first daycare centre in The North East to open a scent room for our daycare dogs, and we opened that for some of the important reasons mentioned above.

Even by hiding some treats within the sand, soil or fallen leaves gives your dog a great outlet which will help build up trust and confidence.

Being outdoors is also a great time to work on your dog's lead and recall training, certainly something a lot of dogs lack.

It doesn't matter where you live or what you have in your surrounding area you can always find something to make your walk an adventure walk. If you check out the Pets2impress YouTube channel, you will see some examples of the adventures we offer to our daycare dogs.

Walks, of course, too need to be varied, i.e. don't just go to the same place every day. By going on different routes or to different locations, you encourage your dog to make more use of those very important natural senses.

During Lockdown I got bored going to the same places, and I kept altering the route I went on with Buddy because I too was getting bored with the same thing day in day out and dogs do too. This is why I am a member of the National Trust because I enjoy being outdoors and I enjoy taking Buddy to new places and trust me he loves it too.

I have always been an outdoors person, and even with Lady, I enjoyed going to different locations, meeting new people and new friends for Lady was an important part of our daily exercise.

Maybe certain owners don't walk their dogs as much as they should, but I am sure everyone deep down knows they should be walking their dog but let us move on to the next part of your dog's routine, a very important part of your dog's day to day life.

3. Training Times

In an ideal world, we should be spending 3-4 times per day for 5-10 minutes training our dogs. This is a massive confidence builder and will massively help to reduce anxiety in your dog. Always start the session with something you know your dog can do reliably well and always end the session with something your dog knows.

In between, start to teach your dog new things. Trust me, when it comes to training your dog you can be as imaginative as you like as longs you and your dog are both having fun, nothing else matters.

Regular training sessions are a great way to reinforce the Nothing in life is free programme, and in fact, it will help encourage your dog to want to work more for things.

During training times you should also implement some form of brain game such as a puzzle game or scent work as the two work hand in hand together, and both will play a huge part in reducing your dog's anxiety levels.

I often advise something I like to call 'recycle the recycling' which basically means if you are about to throw something in the recycle bin STOP and think "can I make this into a brain game for my dog?" The answer is normally yes, and it's so simple to do but has unlimited benefits for your dog.

An example would be a toilet roll tube, cut it up into rings and then interlock those rings together to make a ball shape, post a couple of treats within and bingo you have a homemade brain game.

Seconds to create but lots of fun for your dog. If he destroys it who cares, it was going in the recycling anyway.

During the Lockdown, I introduced a 14 day online challenge for owners to take part in with their dog. Each day they were given a new challenge which involved either teaching a new trick or creating a brain game. The feedback from this challenge was crazy, one client said

"I have absolutely loved taking part in this group challenge. I love my time spent with Paddy teaching him new tricks etc ., and this group has opened up a whole new load

of ideas that I can use and implement on our day to day activity that didn't even cross my mind. I thought it was going to be a real struggle for him during this isolation period with the lack of exercise and stimulation that he is used to on a daily basis. He is used to getting 2/3 good walks per day as well as 2-3 full days at daycare per week , so naturally , I thought he would be bored and bouncing off the walls with energy. Being part of this group has been great for him, teaching him new tricks and doing things such as jumping over toilet rolls has really helped tire him out both physically and mentally. His tail has never stopped wagging , and I've found he is just as tired at night during this time as he was after a busy on the go day."

Now bearing in mind at the beginning of the lockdown, we were restricted to one bit of exercise per day. Because the above owner implemented the training, she learned from the online challenges she still had a tired and happy dog by the end of the day… with less exercise than normal.

To really help reduce your dog's anxiety, to build up confidence and independence, I cannot stress how important regular training sessions are with your dog. Do not forget these too should be varied, so do not just focus on the same training sessions each day, trust me, your dog will get bored. This now moves us on to the next part of the routine.

4. Regular Playtime

As with the training sessions, you want to aim for a minimum of 3-4 playtime sessions per day with your dog, each session being around 5-10 minutes long.

Vary the toys that you play with, and don't forget rule number 1, if the dog wants to engage in some playtime with you, then he needs to work for it and why? Because nothing in life is free!

Buddy, as like most dogs, has numerous toys but I only ever leave out 3-4 at any one time. I rotate these toys every couple of days to give him something new to play with and to keep things fun for him.

During our playtime sessions, I bring out one of his special toys. I then ask him to sit, and once he has, we continue with our play session.

This is a part of the day that Buddy adores, his favourite toy being an old crock which now does not really resemble any form of footwear but he loves it, and I make use of this on numerous occasions, believe it or not, it's my go-to item to get him back to me when he is off lead because when he sees that nothing else matters.

Any form of active play helps keep your dog's heart healthy, keeps the joints lubricated, and improves his overall balance and coordination. Active play sessions also have a huge impact on a dog's mental health, keeping them happy, building confidence and most importantly reducing anxiety.

When choosing toys for your dog always try and aim for ones that encourage your dog to make use of their natural senses for example toys with various textures or toys that can be stuffed with treats such as the Kong range.

Remember playtime should be fun for you and your dog, and it's a great way once again to build on that strong bond you already have with your dog.

We are now ready to move onto the final part of the routine, a very important aspect of any dog's routine.

5 – Quiet time

If you implement the above (which you should), naturally it will tire your dog out a lot more than he is used to; therefore, it is very important that he is able to rest throughout the day. Dog's should have their own space that they can go to for some chill time. This could be a bed or a crate but somewhere where the dog feels safe and secure.

We know what our moods are like if we don't get a good night's sleep, we can be moody, argumentative, angry, emotional… the list goes on. Dog's too, like us, need their sleep.

Imagine what effect it would have on you if your sleep was disturbed every night? I'm a Father of 3, trust me, I know!

If your sleep pattern keeps getting disturbed, then this will have a huge impact on your mental wellbeing and energy levels. A dog that doesn't get enough downtime can become very stressed and anxious, and it can play a massive part on their day to day life and in some cases can lead to aggression as the dog gets frustrated a lot quicker or less tolerant.

Make sure when your dog goes to his bed he is not disturbed, if you have children at home then make sure his sleeping area is away from the children and actively encourage your dog to have a little nap. We will be discussing this further in a later chapter.

Dogs love to know what is coming next and throughout this chapter, we have discussed the foundations of what you need to implement to ensure your dog gains confidence, independence and most importantly a reduction in their anxiety levels.

In the next chapter, we will be looking at the effects diet can have on your dog's day to day life as well as discussing certain remedies that may help reduce your dog's anxiety levels.

Chapter Four

You are what you eat

We have all heard the phrase, you are what you eat, and the same applies to our dogs. I always remember being a young lad and being told I couldn't eat the blue smarties… did you get that too?

These days we are constantly having healthy eating thrown in our face, it is on the TV, on the news, on social media, and why? The reason why is because it is better for us and helps us live longer, happier lives. We care (or should) about what we eat, and although I love my chocolate I do try and have a well-balanced diet, I say that with a box of Maltesers next to me… they help me think, I'm sure you understand.

When it comes to dog food, there is such variation and so much conflicting information, how on earth do you know what to choose? I do not plan on telling you the ins and outs of diet foods available for dogs in this book, but one thing I would say is to avoid any diets that have meat or animal derivatives listed in their ingredients. These diets are normally classed as mixed formulated.

What is meant by the term meat and animal derivatives?

"Meat and animal derivatives are legally defined in the Animal Feed Regulations 2019. PFMA members use by-products of the human food industry that come from animals slaughtered under veterinary supervision, e.g. Heart, lung, or muscle meat, which may not be traditionally eaten by people in this country" – www.pfma.org.uk

Unfortunately, these diet foods normally equivalate to us eating fast food every day. Let us be honest, fast food is normally quite yummy but long term that's not going to have a huge impact on our health and wellbeing and over time it's going to make us feel pretty rubbish and pretty sluggish. A lot of the ingredients found in cheaper dog foods are not of the highest quality, and correct me if I am wrong, but we only want the best for our dog, right?

Help! My Dog Doesn't Like Being Left Alone

I would advise speaking to your veterinary practice, and I am sure they will help guide you in the right direction and help you make the right decision for your dog.

I can hold my hands up, initially I fed Lady a low-quality cheap diet food. This was the man training to be a veterinary nurse; therefore, I should have known better, but the truth be told I was on minimum wage, I lived alone, I had bills to pay, food to buy and I just found it more convenient to pick up Lady's food from the supermarket when I was picking up my shopping plus it was cheaper.

It wasn't until I trained as a nutrition advisor that I realised just how important diet is and the impacts it can have on a dog's stress and anxiety levels. Before the children arrived, I used to work crazy hours. I would get up at 5:30am and sometimes not get home again until 10pm. I found it easier to pick up a burger and chips from a fast food restaurant to eat on the go. Guaranteed by the weekend I was feeling sluggish, couldn't be bothered and on the odd days I did have off, all I wanted to do was sit in front of the TV with my feet up.

Recently I have invested in a PT, and yes, I do still eat my chocolate. I have my set meals, and I make sure I track what I eat and make sure to eat more healthy throughout the week. As a result of that, I have felt more energised, more alert and a lot less sluggish, and it certainly played a massive part on my day to day mood.

Maybe you are not exactly what you eat; otherwise, I would be a box of Maltesers right now, but diet does play a huge role in our lives, and it does with your dog's lives too.

Are you buying your dog cheap diet food? Are you picking up your food from a supermarket?

Maybe it is time to change that?

There are a number of diet foods available on the market specifically designed to help improve your dog's behaviour and to maintain an optimal emotional balance which in turn will help your dog overcome the day to day stresses life can have. These specific diets have all of the vital amino acids and vitamins required to synthesise the necessary neurotransmitters in a dog's brain to help promote calmness and relaxation.

Herbal Remedies – to Add a Little Extra Calmness

Just like us, every now and then we may need something to help chill us out (no, I don't mean anything illegal!). There are a number of herbal remedies available for dogs that come in tablets, sprays, collars and plugins to help them deal and cope with everyday life. These can be supplemented alongside your dog's diet and can have a number of benefits. It is important to remember, though, that these are not magic pills or sprays that cure-all. They are aimed to work alongside a training programme. Just like diet pills, if you read the small print, they require a healthy diet and exercise too

Choosing the Right Herbal Remedy for Your Dog

If you go to your local pet shop, I am sure they will have a number of herbal remedies available which can be quite daunting, which one do you choose? If you go to one pet shop, you may be advised one thing, if you then visit another pet shop, they may advise you something completely different.

I personally think the best place to go is your veterinary practice. The veterinary staff will all have had training regarding the products they are selling and advising, and chances are, the staff will have used them on their dogs before… having worked in practice for a number of years I know vets, vet nurses and veterinary receptionists all have the 'problematic dogs'.

I would always prefer to give my dog something that has been advised by a veterinary practice because at the end of the day these guys have undergone a lot of training to be where they are, and from my point of view, their opinion matters.

Of course, you can go on social media and ask everyone else for their opinion, but in all honesty, these guys are not vets or vet nurses.

Where do you go to get your car fixed? A mechanic! Where do you go if you are unwell? A doctor! Why is this? These are professionals in that field and although I am sure the people you ask on social media may generally want to help, let's be honest they are not veterinary trained. As a canine behaviourist, I only recommend products that can be purchased from a veterinary practice and having used them myself with my dogs in the past, I know they help.

Let us get one thing clear though, introducing herbal remedies to your dog's diet is not going to correct the problem; certainly, it may help, but it certainly won't make your dog think "oooh I do not mind being left alone". The idea of herbal remedies is to help reduce your dog's anxiety so that you can introduce changes and a training plan to help correct the problem.

When my wife was due our first baby, I made sure to stock up on the old herbal remedies to give to Lady before and after the baby arrived. This was going to be a huge change for her and I wanted to make sure she had some additional support alongside the other forms of training I was implementing to prepare her for the arrival of a newborn baby and the training that I put in after the baby was born.

A lot of owners believe that when they get these happy pills from the veterinary practice, all will be sunshine and roses and the dog will happily cope being left alone, but life sadly is not that simple.

Of course, a good quality diet will help and by supplementing herbal remedies you may find that too helps but in order the help build up confidence and independence when left alone we need to move on and put together a plan of action to help your dog cope being left alone.

This is exactly what we will be doing in the next chapter, but before you move on, it is important to digest the information from the previous chapters and make sure you are implementing these new changes into your dog's day to day life.

Chapter Five

Teaching your dog to settle

When I get home on a night time after work, I like to settle the kids and then go downstairs and put my feet up whilst watching some TV before bed. This is what I would class as my relaxing time.

Others would choose to soak in a nice hot bath, read a book in bed, sit in the garden with a glass of wine etc. the truth is we all have our own ways of relaxing and de-stressing.

Dogs need somewhere to relax as well, and if we have any hope of leaving them alone, we need to make sure they have a place that is comfortable, relaxing and most importantly safe for them.

This area should not be somewhere you send your dog to for 'being naughty' or to 'calm them down' because remember we praise the good and ignore the bad, we shouldn't need to correct the unwanted behaviours because we should be putting our efforts into praising what we would class as good, isn't that right… I can hear you all saying "yes, Tim".

So how do we teach the dog to be calm and settle?

- Begin by placing the dog's bed in the area you plan to leave your dog in when you are not home, this will need to be somewhere different to where you are currently leaving your dog (more on that later on in the book).
- Calmly take the dog to his bed. The key is to not force him but instead use a lure such as a treat and lure him to his bed.
- When he has all four paws on the bed reward him with a treat.
- Practice makes perfect so keep practising and practising and then start to introduce a command word such as 'bed'.
- You want to eventually aim to be able to reduce the lure, and you should be able to send the dog to his bed by command word only.

- Work at building on the distance at which you ask your dog to go to bed from. So initially you will use the lure to encourage the dog to his bed, but eventually, you should be able to point say from one end of the room, issue the command and off the dog goes, knowing something good is going to come.
- Once the dog understands what his bed is, and he understands that going there gets him a reward, we now need to get him to settle on his bed.
- You need to look for changes in the dog's respiration, body posture and facial expressions to assess the relaxation in your dog.
- Send your dog to their bed and request a 'sit' or a 'down'.
- Give the word of your choosing for relaxation but say it only once, repeating over and over will only confuse your dog.
- Pick a targeted behaviour to watch and then reward the dog with a treat and praise for displaying that calmness behaviour.
- Get the dog up, move him away and then send him back to his bed and repeat the exercise.
- Sessions should be short and sweet and always aim for success.

Once your dog happily settles, we can then look at asking the dog to stay in their new bed. The aim of the next exercise is to stop your dog following you everywhere around the house so you can actually go to the toilet in peace or have a nice soak without him peering his head over the bath watching your every move.

Do not get me wrong it is fine to allow them to follow you around the house at times as dogs are naturally curious and they are keen to know what you are up to however we need to make sure they do not act like our shadow as we want them to have the confidence and independence to be able to settle in a room whilst we are in another room. Most importantly we also need to make sure they are getting the fifth part of their routine, quiet time.

If they can't do this, how can we possibly expect them to settle when we need to leave the house?

When teaching the stay command always start small and do not be afraid to take baby steps, after all, we want to get this right and as the old saying goes, slow and steady always wins the race!

Teaching the stay command

- Send the dog to his bed.
- Request the dog to settle.
- Ask the dog to stay.
- Issue a flat palm towards the dog to indicate you want the dog to stay.
- Take one step away from the dog and then go straight back and praise the dog when you return.
- Practice a number of times and then start taking two steps away from the dog before returning and then three steps, four steps, five steps etc.
- Eventually, you should be able to leave the room.

Over time you will be able to build up how many steps you can take away from the dog before returning and then you can start to increase the amount of time you stay away as well, so you can start to enjoy those lovely soaks in the bath without your beloved pooch staring at you the entire time.

If your dog is literally your shadow, then of course, this is going to take some time but try not to rush this stage and certainly do not skip it our because we need our dogs to be able to settle indoors when we are home before we attempt to ask them to settle when we leave.

Once you are at the stay stage of this training, make sure you use it at every opportunity to really try and reinforce that behaviour. For example, if you need to go and put the kettle on or top up your glass of wine (I am not here to judge) or if you need to pop to the toilet these are all perfect opportunities to practice getting your dog to stay.

Eventually, you want to try and aim to close a door on your dog so for example if the dog's bed is in the living room and you need to pop upstairs to go to the toilet, send the dog to his bed, ask him to stay and then shut the door. You will need to work on this slowly do not just do it out of the blue as this could cause your dog to get distressed and knock back the training you have worked so hard to achieve.

It is important to mention again that the dog's bed should be a positive place, make sure you never send the dog there as a punishment, do not

Help! My Dog Doesn't Like Being Left Alone

do training sessions if you are stressed or tired as we want the dog to associate this area with positive things. If your dog has a bed and you have used it as a punishment area in the past, then maybe now is the time to replace that bed and start afresh.

The key to success is to practice at a time when your dog is more likely to be already relaxing and if needs be do not be afraid to give your dog a food stuffed toy, such as a Kong toy, to help keep them occupied during longer periods of absence.

It is good practice to try and ask your dog to settle during distractions as well such as cooking, housework, visitors coming round.

It will be very tempting during this time for your dog to get up and investigate what is going on and this is where we give the dog the opportunity to learn for themselves to be calm and to relax. We ignore the unwanted behaviours and wait until they settle again, when they do make sure to be ready with a reward.

I can easily settle when given the chance. I love nothing more than putting my feet up and watching TV, but I am not as curious as our canine friends and certainly not as needy as some of them.

Some dogs just want to be by our sides every second of every day, and the only way they will settle is if they are touching us in some way or another, whether that is lying on top of us or resting their head on our feet.

Let's be honest, that is extremely cute, but it is not helping build up any confidence or independence, and that's what we need our dogs to have if we have any chance of them settling when left alone.

It is important that you take your time with this lesson and go at a pace that suits your dog, so you must initially work on the bed command, then request the dog to settle, then request the dog to stay as you move around the house, increase the time you are able to be away from your dog and then start to increase distractions to really try and reinforce the settle and stay.

Do not be afraid to give the dog something to keep them occupied as this will reinforce the positive vibe we are wanting the dog to have about his new bed. When you are confident that your dog is happily settling down, then you can start to practice with closing the door behind you, just remember to take your time with that stage of the training as for some dogs this can be too much, especially if rushed.

Once our dog is able to settle in the house and we are now free to pee and poop in peace or even have a soak in the bath with a glass of wine and some music, we can now look at moving on to the next stage, and that involves uncoupling departure cues or triggers as I like to call them from departure, i.e. you leaving the house.

Please do not move on though until your dog will happily settle in his new bed… remember Rome was not built in a day!

Chapter Six

Identifying the triggers

Dogs are incredible little creatures, and they are very good at predicting what will come next, including predicting when we are about to leave them. No, they are not psychic, but they are able to pick up on certain triggers that we do, such as putting on our shoes or certain triggers we display through our body language. They can also learn from experience that you doing this can then lead to that which can then lead to you leaving the house.

Let me give you an example. I have lived in my house for ten years now, and when Lady was still with us, her lead always lived in the cupboard under the stairs. Now, I could have gone to that cupboard 100 times a day and Lady would not so much as even lift her head, however, if it was her walk time and I were to approach that cupboard to get her lead to take her for a walk, boy did she let me know she was excited. Her tail would wag, she bounced up and down, and she chattered away in her adorable German Shephard voice (no I am not going mad, German Shepard owners will understand).

I found it fascinating that she knew that it was her walk time, and I was interested to find out what it was I was doing that she associated with going for a walk. Now, I am a man that likes answers; therefore, I decided to experiment with certain things, and I did a number of experiments to try and trick Lady to see if I could get her excited when it wasn't actually her walk time. It sounds a bit mean when I say it like that, but I am the sort of person that likes to find answers or triggers that cause a dog to display certain behaviours, that's my job after all.

I went to the cupboard in my dressing gown and picked up her lead, she lifted her head, but she didn't bounce off the walls in excitement. On other occasions, I went to the cupboard in my dog walking clothes but never reached for her lead.

I then tried going at different times of the day to assess Lady's reaction. Maybe I had too much time on my hands, but I was very curious to find out what got her so excited apart from me actually saying the W-word.

The truth is I would have displayed certain triggers that led up to Lady going for a walk, and over time Lady would have associated those actions with the fact she was about to go for a walk.

So during my experiments, because I was not following that particular order of events (the triggers that Lady had gotten used to), Lady did not react. Yes she lifted her head to see what I was doing if I were to pick up her lead, but chances are she was just showing an interest just in case she missed something else… make sense?

Now, this didn't happen overnight, Lady would have spent time watching what I did and with the repetition, she soon associated the order of events and the actions I took with the fact it was her walk time. So, for example, before I took Lady for her walk I would always go for my final wee (sorry I know, too much information), I would then come downstairs and put on my shoes and dog walking coat.

I leave out the back when I walk the dog, so I always check the front door is locked, I then stock my pocket with treats and poop bags before going to the cupboard for the lead.

We all have our own little rituals and things we do before we leave the house, and there could have been things I did way before going for my final wee that Lady picked up on, even something as simple as having a drink (non-alcoholic may I add) before going for my final wee and because I tend to follow this same routine each time I am going for a walk, Lady soon started to connect the dots and realised walk time was coming.

Just as Lady was able to predict when I was taking her for a walk, she was also able to predict when I was going to leave her and trust me, your dog will also know as they will be watching your every movement and you too will have your own little routine that you follow before you leave home, and over time your dog will start to connect the dots just as Lady did.

This association does not happen overnight it takes time for any dog to build that connection but once a dog realises that you doing this, is then followed by that, you then do this, and when you leave they can start to show signs of feeling stressed and anxious before you have even left the house.

To help you understand better, let's look again into my weekday morning routine, followed by my weekend morning routine. I know I touched upon this in a previous chapter, but I want you to understand just how clever our dogs are at picking up on these triggers due to learning and repetition.

Weekday Routine

- Once the alarm has gone off, I get straight up (no time to hit the snooze button in this house).
- I go for my morning wee (sorry again).
- I then go downstairs and put Buddy out for his morning wee.
- Whilst Buddy is out, I get myself a drink of juice.
- I then bring Buddy back in and head upstairs to brush my teeth and to put on my dog walking clothes.
- I then come back down and take Buddy for his morning walk.
- On our return, I feed Buddy, then empty the dishwasher and put a load in the washing machine.
- I then head upstairs for a shower and to get ready for work.
- Once ready, I go back downstairs, and I grab some breakfast, which is normally a yoghurt or a piece of fruit.
- I quickly gather some snacks for work.
- I then put on my shoes, coat, get my car keys and then off I go.

This is my weekday routine which is exactly the same every day I am at work. The only time it may slightly change would be if the kids woke up the same time as me. As I write it down though, I do appear to go up and downstairs a number of times, maybe I need to look at changing my routine, so I do have some time to hit the snooze button.

My weekend routine is similar to my weekday routine but also very different.

Weekend Routine

- I normally wake up when the kids wake up (sadly this is not much later than if I were getting up for work... anyone got any tips on getting the kids to sleep longer?)
- I go for my morning wee (once again, sorry for the too much information).
- I then go downstairs and put Buddy out for his morning wee.
- I still pour myself a drink of juice, and I then bring Buddy back in.
- I then go upstairs, brush my teeth and quickly put on my dog walking clothes and take Buddy for his first walk of the day.
- When we return, I have breakfast with the kids (normally in front of the TV as a weekend treat and normally not much more than a yoghurt or a piece of fruit).
- I tend to potter for the first part of the morning, empty the dishwasher, tidy up after breakfast, enjoy a bit time with the kids.
- It's normally a couple of hours after I have returned with Buddy that I go for my morning shower and get ready for the day.

So, from my weekday to my weekend routine there are certain things you can see that I do routinely, i.e. I always have my morning wee as soon as I get up out of bed and I always go down and see to Buddy and take him for his walk however weekdays tend to be a lot more rushed whereas weekends are a lot more chilled.

The order of events is very different to that of my weekday events and albeit I do a lot of things in my weekend routine that I do in my weekday routine such as emptying the dishwasher, having a drink of juice, brushing my teeth and having a shower but these are not in the same order as they are during my weekday routine.

Buddy tends to come to work with me most days, so he isn't left in a morning, and the days he doesn't come with me he goes up for a cuddle in bed with the Mrs but regardless if he comes with me or not my morning routine never changes, I am a man of routine.

This routine was also very similar when Lady was alive as well which is why over time, Lady would have started to connect the dots and seeing me emptying the dishwasher, having breakfast, heading upstairs for a shower, coming back down in my uniform as signs that I was about to leave her.

Some dogs will literally follow their owners around the house watching their every movement, and I would probably say (just judging from my wife's routine) that ladies will display a lot more triggers such as doing their hair, putting on their makeup etc. etc… ladies spend more time making an effort whereas I just want to get out the house… I am a what you see is what you get kind of guy.

It doesn't matter what your routine is, it may be similar to mine it may be completely different, but one thing is for sure, your dog will have over time built a connection to your routine and learnt through association that they are about to be left and a lot of dogs will show signs to say they are feeling stressed or anxious way before you have even left them. These signs could include

- Pacing (as previously mentioned)
- Following owners around the house
- Yawning
- Shaking
- Whimpering

Lady used to display a number of these behaviours when I was getting ready but very interestingly on a weekend she watched what I was doing, but once she realised I was not following my normal routine, she settled down as she never felt the need to worry further at this stage.

As we all have our own routines for getting up in a morning and going to work we also have a routine (even if we are not aware of it) of what we do say if we need to pop to the shops or if we are going out with our friends. Your dog may not pick up on these routines as confidently as they do with our morning routine, but that's more than likely because we don't do it as frequently, whereas getting up and going to work in most people's cases is Monday – Friday giving the dog plenty of opportunities to connect those dots.

So what you need to do is look at your morning routine and pay attention to what you do when you get up in a morning, and you need to watch your dog and monitor their behaviours as well.

Make a note (written or mental) of what it is that you do that potentially triggers off your dog to display signs of feeling stressed or anxious. It may be earlier on in your routine, but it may be the very end of your morning routine, i.e. putting on your work uniform, putting on your shoes, coat, getting your key etc. By observing your dog's behaviour during your day to day routine and comparing it to days that you are not going to leave them, you will soon be able to identify what activities you undertake that triggers your dog to feel anxious or stressed.

Make a note of these triggers, and whatever triggers you may find that your dog reacts too. We now need to look at uncoupling those departure cues from an actual departure, and that will take a little bit of time and patience but here is how you do it.

To uncouple those departure cues from an actual departure, we need the dog to stop thinking you doing a certain activity means you are going to leave so for example, pick up your keys and walk to the door. It is important at this stage we do not exit, but instead, we wait for a few moments and then return the keys to their normal place and go and sit back down.

Do similar activities with your coat, pick up your coat, put it on and go to the front door and wait for a few moments before taking it off again, hanging it up and then going to sit down. On other occasions, put on your coat and then go and sit down and put the television on. I appreciate this may not be ideal in summer months but trust me it's what you need to do.

Now the next suggestion may be a bit unpopular as most people want to forget about work when they are off however something simple that you can do is to put on your uniform on your day off and sit and watch some television with it on.

The purpose of the above is to take away that association your dog has built with these activities, and by doing these, your dog will eventually not associate you wearing your uniform or picking up your keys, putting on your shoes, putting on your coat etc. as a sign that you about to leave them; therefore, reducing any initial potential stress your dog may be used to feeling.

We need to keep sessions short and sweet so for example, do not get up, put on your coat, walk to the front door, wait a few moments and then return your coat followed by picking up your keys or putting on your shoes. The aim is to work on these triggers individually and take your time. Whether you are teaching your dog to sit, walk nicely on a lead or be able to cope when being left alone, you must remember the rules of patience and consistency.

The purpose of identifying triggers and uncoupling them from departures is to prevent your dog from getting stressed before you actually leave and there are certain behaviours you need to look out for during these training sessions. These behaviours need to be avoided, and they include an increase in anxiety when the trigger is presented, inability to settle in between presentations of the triggers or the dog following and watching your every move.

If you notice any of the above, it is important to stop, take a rest and go at a much slower pace the next time you practice.

I want you to get this right as I want your dog to feel better when he/she is left alone therefore you need to take your time with each of these stages and do not progress until you have mastered the previous stage.

The aim of this stage is to ensure that we uncouple departure cues from an actual departure and no longer cause the dog to respond with anxiety. So, to conclude, we need to begin by identifying the trigger points which may involve some observing over a couple of days, watching what your dog does as you get ready and make a note of which stage of your routine does your dog start to show signs of distress.

Once you have identified the triggers, you can then start to change the dog's association to these certain triggers by wearing your shoes indoors, sitting with your coat on when watching television, wearing your uniform on days you are not at work etc.

It will take a little bit of time and some patience, but eventually, your dog will stop associating these activities with the fact you are about to leave them.

We will soon be moving on to some planned training departures to build up the time the dog can be left alone, but first I want to look at changing where we are leaving our dog when left alone.

Chapter Seven

Changing the place where you leave your dog

Now to understand why I want you to change the location where you leave your dog, I want to share with you an experience that happened to me back in July 2019.

It was a lovely sunny day, and I was out with my three children, Sienna, Harvey and Darcey. My oldest two, Sienna and Harvey, were on their scooters as they generally do when we go out. I decided to dare my oldest daughter to scooter down a very steep bank (please do not judge me), and I promised her a game of mini-golf in return for her bravery.

I used to scooter down that same bank when I was her age, and I always remember it being great fun. Now Sienna is a wise child and clearly thought sod that for fish and chips and she said, "Daddy, if you do it first then I will", smart move from my child if I do say so myself.

Naturally, if I expected my daughter to do it, I too was going to have to do it; as mentioned, I always used to do it when I was younger and that's the key part… when I was younger not as a 34-year grown man.

So, I took my daughter's pink scooter, and I ventured halfway up the bank, I was trying to be brave, not stupid. My son, Harvey followed me up with his 3-wheel scooter. Now the kids always wear helmets, knee pads and elbow pads just to be on the safe side. I, however, had Buddy's treat bag wrapped around my side, I was wearing shorts, a t-shirt and some TOMS (for those that do not know these are a form of footwear that very easily slip off).

I looked at Harvey who was egging me on to go, and he certainly has no fear, so he too was going to attempt this ridiculously steep bank.

I will always remember the feeling I had when I set off, the scooter very quickly picked up speed and my initial thought was, "Shit, I'm not going to stop, this is going too fast", forgetting that there was a brake on the back of the scooter and had I just moved my foot backwards and pressed it I would have stopped with no concerns however that's not quite what happened.

I decided to make the big mistake of taking my foot off to try and stop myself, now bearing in mind I was travelling at a very high speed, me taking off a foot was probably not the best course of action to take which I sharply realised as my foot twisted backwards and off I fell, crashing to the ground.

My first instinct was thinking oh god, my son is attempting that very same bank on his scooter, I knew I was bleeding, and I sensed I was sore here, there and everywhere but at this stage, my priority was to ensure Harvey was ok.

It turns out he was fine, he managed to stop himself halfway because guess what, he used his bloody brakes! He had fallen to his knees, but because he had his knee pads on, he was fine, thankfully… I'll not be winning any Father of the year awards.

I then looked back to see where my daughter's scooter had gone to see a bunch of people laughing, including my daughter, who found this whole experience highly amusing.

The bag, I was wearing with Buddy's treats and poop bags, had exploded everywhere, so my second gut instinct was to collect all of the poop bags and treats as people were walking past, laughing and generally taking the piss… in all fairness, I too would have probably done the same thing.

I then rallied up the kids and quickly hurried out of the park, with blood dripping down my sides. Once I had hobbled home, I realised that I had a number of injuries and once the embarrassment and adrenaline had slowly disappeared, I realised I was in quite a bit of pain, and I noticed my wrist had begun to swell up.

Ideally, then would have been the correct time to go to the hospital but I was home alone with the kids, the wife was visiting friends in York so she couldn't get home in a hurry.

Now I did redeem myself for trying to encourage the kids to scooter down the bank because I still took them to mini-golf, despite the fact I was in a lot of pain.

Help! My Dog Doesn't Like Being Left Alone

When the wife returned home, she seen how swollen my arm and wounds were and sent me straight off to hospital and instructed me not to come back until I had been seen.

With 14% battery and a 4-hour minimum wait at A and E, the day just was not getting any better.

The nurse that triaged me was actually someone I went to school with so I had to explain the whole thing to her too, and after a long wait, an examination and an X-ray, it turned out I had broken my arm.

With a busy week ahead, this was not the news I wanted to hear, but I only had one person to blame, that would be me!

Now it took a long time for that break to heal and after numerous trips to the physiotherapist, my wrist finally healed.

I am not telling you this story to give you a good giggle, although I would not blame you if you did, it wasn't one of my finest moments. Let's just say I train dogs much better than I do riding a scooter.

The reason I am telling you this story is because it took me until the following June before I tried to ride my daughter's scooter again and when I did, I felt very unsteady and uneasy and sharply gave it back to her.

As a child, I was always on my scooter and never had any fear, but I guess as you get older you do develop more fears of certain things, or maybe you just get wiser who knows. My main concern was that I was going to fall off again and that incident we shall call it came flooding back. Do not get me wrong we all have a good laugh about it, but that negative association I created as a result of that said incident had clearly stuck with me.

If you have a negative association with something, it takes time to build up a positive association which is why I suggest that you change where you leave your dog when left home alone.

By now, your dog will more than likely have built up a negative association to the room he is left in when you are not there, chances are he avoids that room unless you are in there with him. This is certainly something I have seen with dog's I have worked with in the past.

We want to teach our dog that he will be ok being left alone and we want to try and make that as positive as possible. By starting off on a negative, you are kind of setting yourself up to fail.

Now here is the tricky part and I will explain more later on in the book when you are working on teaching your dog to settle you will use the new location that you plan to leave your dog in eventually. When it comes to building up gradual departures, again you will use the new location, but if say during a training session you are able to leave your dog for 15 minutes, but you know you need to go out and you will be longer than that 15 minutes, then the dog should go back into the original room he was left in.

The purpose of that is to prevent creating a negative association with the new chosen area.

We have to go to work, we have to go to the shops, we cannot stay at home with our dog 24/7, and building up departure times will take some patience, and it may take some time, so it is very important that we do not risk creating a negative association with the newly chosen place. This place should be fun. You should feed your dog here, give your dog treats here, leave your dog's toys here etc.

This is certainly not a place where we send the dog if he is being 'naughty' or acting problematically and in order to get the success we want this new chosen area needs to be a fun and positive area for your dog.

So apart from embarrassing myself further by sharing the story of the time I fell off my daughter's scooter we also discussed during this chapter the importance of creating a new positive environment for your dog to stay during your absence and why we should move your dog away from the original space, where by now, no doubt, he would have created a negative association.

Still with me? Good, because now we move onto building up the time you are able to leave your dog alone with gradual departures.

Chapter Eight

Gradual Departures

So far we have covered a lot within this book from the nothing in life is free programme, to triggers, to getting your dog to settle on command etc. It is extremely important that you do not rush stages and you work on those stages first before attempting to move on to gradual departures. If we want our dog to be calm when we leave them, we need to make sure we build this up slowly. Therefore, you must begin by working through the previous chapters within this book and only when your dog is ready should you move on to this chapter.

In the previous chapter, we discussed how important it is to have a training area and a non-training area.

The training area will be the new chosen location where you plan to leave your dog, and this will be the area you work on building up gradual departures.

The non – training area will be the area you use outside of training sessions so for example if you have built up a departure time of 30 minutes, but you need to leave the house for 45 minutes the dog should be placed in the non-training area (the original place where he normally goes when you leave him).

If you had built up a departure time of 30 minutes and you needed to leave the house for 20 minutes, then the dog would be left in the new location. Got it? Good, let's move on.

So where do we begin?

Stage One –

Send the dog to his bed in the new chosen area that you wish him to be when you leave. Once there, you need to follow your routine for leaving but when you get to the front door, stop, turn around, take off your coat, shoes, put down your keys and then go and sit down.

Check for any signs of distress from your dog. If you notice the dog appears unsettled or unhappy then chances are, he is not ready for this stage, and you need to do further work on previous lessons. Do not ever be afraid or disheartened to take a step back; if your dog needs more time, he needs more time.

This should be practised a couple of times a day, and it is important that you try and keep these pretend departures as lifelike as possible, even if that means going to the toilet when you really do not need to go.

Stage Two –

Stage two is a repetition of stage one, however this time you are actually going to open the front door and step outside and then guess what, you stop, turn around, take off your coat, shoes, put down your keys and go back indoors and sit down or continue with what you were doing before the training session.

Sessions need to be short and sweet, and as in stage one, you should aim to practice this a couple of times per day.

Stage Three –

Within this stage, we continue with what we did within stage one and two, but this time we close the front door and lock it behind us. I am sure by now you can guess what happens next?

You guessed it, unlock the door, go back indoors, take off your shoes, coat and put back down your keys and then continue with whatever it was you were doing before you began the training session.

Stage Four –

Moving on from stage three, we now, once locking the front door, can take a walk to the front gate and then, yes, you guessed correctly once again, stop, turn around, unlock the front door, go back indoors, take off your coat, shoes, put down your keys and then continue with whatever it is you were doing before the training session.

Do I really need to continue with stage five? Basically, we are aiming at building up very slowly the amount of time we leave our dog for. Initial-

Help! My Dog Doesn't Like Being Left Alone

ly departures must be very short (seconds) but eventually those seconds can then move to minutes and then those minutes will eventually move to hours (obviously not exceeding the 4-hour rule).

It is extremely important that you return within the designated time, do not stay away longer even if you feel your dog is doing ok, once again, slow and steady always wins the race!

You must remember to keep your departures as lifelike as possible, so I would advise re-looking at your day to day routine and make a mental note of what you do just before you leave the house as during training sessions this is what you need to be doing.

We need the dog to believe you are genuinely leaving the house, but by doing it gradually you teach the dog that you will be returning, and by taking your time you will ultimately help your dog cope when being left alone, as opposed to stressing and worrying that you are not coming home.

When you build up your departure times, you should only look at increasing the length of absence if no pre-departure anxiety is seen, and no excitement or anxiety on return is evident.

Always space the training sessions out throughout the day and only practice when your dog is calm and relaxed. There is no benefit in doing multiple sessions in a row.

You will find that your initial progress is very slow before your dog can be left alone and this is certainly one of the lengthy elements of teaching a dog to cope being left alone, but if you rush this stage, then you are setting yourself and your dog up for failure.

One more time, slow and steady always wins the race and do not forget your dog should be calm when you depart and when you return for the training plan to be successful.

When I was building up my departure times when working with Lady, I tended to do more on a weekend when I was off work, and I was lucky in the fact I got one day off in the week as well, so I used these days to do more training with her.

If the truth be told, I didn't want to do any practice with Lady and her departure times when I had been out at work already that day. I wanted to get home and chill and spend some time with her; however, I did make use of the settle command when getting a bath and when preparing my tea and I still made sure she got some training sessions before bed.

I guess there is no right or wrong answer on when you should practice, but the more practice you put in, the quicker you get the results. You just have to remember the golden rules of this chapter, when doing training sessions, you place your dog in the new area that you wish your dog to be left when alone and when doing non-training sessions the dog gets placed back in the original room.

The reason we do this is to prevent the dog building up a negative association with the new room. We want the new area to be fun, comfortable and positive and we cannot take any risks with that one.

So, providing you have worked on previous chapters, you can then move onto gradual departures and building up slowly the amount of time you can leave your dog for, starting with seconds, then minutes and then hours.

Now we can move on to some of the do's and don'ts, which we have already touched upon the many things I did wrong with Lady so let us look at what we should be doing.

Chapter Nine

The dos and the don'ts

Many would think that the key to success involves working on the gradual departure times; however, that is only a small part of fixing the actual problem. We must make sure we keep our dogs happy, build confidence and reduce anxiety.

We covered all of that at the beginning of the book, and it is important that you continue with that, even when you are able to leave your dog for a decent amount of time. Now it is time to look at the do's and don'ts when leaving our dog alone as many, including me tend to make a lot of mistakes along the way which in a lot of cases can create further issues with your dog's behaviour when left alone.

Saying Goodbye Before You Leave

I would say, as humans, this comes naturally to us to say goodbye when we leave. I never leave the house without giving the kids a big kiss, cuddle and tell them to be kind, make good choices and I that I will see them after I finish work.

I used to do the same to Lady; naturally, I changed the wording of my goodbye. Normally it would go something like this

"I'm just going to work. I won't be long, be good."

I used to say this every time I was going to leave her home alone. Now and then I may have mixed it up a bit however them main words "I won't be long" and "be good" would always be included within the sentence and I was guaranteed to say those words once I had her secure in the kitchen.

I never said those words when I went to bed, or if I needed to go to the toilet or if I wanted to go for a bath. I only said those words when I was about to leave the house without Lady. So, what happened? Those words became a trigger, and Lady started to associate those words with the fact she was going to be left alone.

I will always remember when I got in touch with a canine behaviourist to ask for some help with Lady. At this time, I felt like a complete failure; however, he soon put my mind at rest, and I am very glad I did get in touch with him, and I am glad I followed the advice he gave me because it worked.

He came out to do an assessment, and he asked me to follow my normal routine of leaving Lady alone so that is what I did, and this is certainly something I ask my clients to do when I do any home assessments because I like to get a full picture of how the dog is feeling prior to the owner leaving, what happens once the owner leaves and what happens once the owner returns.

After the initial assessment we discussed my routine, and he said I needed to stop saying goodbye to Lady. In fact, I needed to ignore her for 10-15 minutes before I left and 10-15 minutes once I returned.

Boy was that tough, and it took some time to train myself not to do it but it is necessary as we want the dog to learn that your comings and goings are no big deal.

Can I Give My Dog a Treat When I Leave?

Without fail, I always gave Lady a Kong toy or a natural chew before I left her and I do the same with Buddy now. I think it is nice that they have something to keep them occupied when I am not there plus the benefit of giving the dog something to chew means 1. They are not chewing my furniture, and 2. Power chewing can relieve stress for many dogs.

I would say the issue a lot of owners make is they only give the dog the Kong toy when they are about to leave, therefore making the Kong toy another trigger.

Therefore, it is fine to give the dog a Kong but make sure he gets a Kong during the day when you are home as well to avoid the dog seeing this as another sign you are about to leave them alone.

Some dogs will not eat when left alone as they find the experience of being alone too much, and if that's the case, you need to be working more on your triggers, the settle command and the gradual departures.

Leave Your Dog With an Item of Clothing That Smells Like You

A used towel or an old t-shirt that you have slept in recently can work wonders.

Just like babies' dogs too can benefit from this as it offers familiarity and emotes positive feelings such as comfort and love.

In all fairness, I did this from day one of leaving Lady alone, and in the early days I did come back to my dressing gown being full of dog poop… luckily, I had a spare.

I know Lady liked my dressing gown because if I ever took it off and threw it on the floor if I got too hot, she would be there quicker than a flash of lightning and although she was a big clumsy German Shephard, she managed to curl up into the tiniest ball to make sure all parts of her were touching the dressing gown.

Walk Your Dog Before You Leave and When You Get Home

Remember, of course, to make these walks into adventure walks to try and burn some excess energy off your dog before you leave. I would advise walking your dog when you return home as well. Both will help disassociate the act with departure from your routine.

By burning off some excess energy, the aim is you leave your dog tired, which will hopefully help them settle when you leave.

I appreciate that is going to mean waking up earlier in a morning which is not always ideal; however, surely that has to be better than going to work knowing your dog is stressed? Am I right? Once again, I can hear you saying "yes Tim".

It is important to stress that a little short walk around the block is not going to be sufficient, your dog needs a decent walk, especially if you are planning on leaving them for a couple of hours alone.

Putting on the Radio or Television As You Leave

I do not see any issues with this; however, it is important, especially if using the radio, that this does not just go on when you leave your dog alone. Otherwise, that's right, you guessed it, there is yet again another trigger point.

My wife was forever leaving classical music on for Buddy when she left to which I had to correct her… I had learnt my lesson from Lady.

We are not a family that routinely listens to classical music so had I not intervened; Buddy could have potentially associated that with the fact we were about to leave him so as you can imagine that sharply changed.

The television is slightly different because 9/10 people watch the television on a night time or keep it on during the day for background noise. Therefore, the dog does not necessarily associate that as a cue that you are about to leave.

Should I Punish My Dog When I Return?

As I already mentioned previously within this book, punishment serves no purpose apart from the fact there is a very good chance it could make the situation worse.

I appreciate and totally understand what it is like to get home after a long day at work to notice your dog has destroyed your house, peed and pooped everywhere or to get a knock on the door from your neighbour to say your dog has been howling all day.

It is frustrating, and it is stressful, but equally, you have to remember it is not your dog's fault, they too have had a very stressful day.

The best bit of advice I can give, and certainly something that worked for me, is when you arrive home before going to see to the dog, stop and count to 10.

Just remember whatever it is he/she has done can be cleaned up, no it's not ideal, but that's why you have read this book so that we can work towards correcting these issues.

Should I Get Another Dog?

Put it this way, I had another dog, Pip, and that made no difference whatsoever to Lady's behaviour. We have to remember your dog is experiencing separation anxiety from you and your absence. Having a second dog may help, but there is no guarantee, so please ignore what you read on the internet. In the past, I have always had two dogs, but I would never get another dog to try and correct an ongoing problem, I would work with that problem first.

Imagine getting a second dog that always develops separation anxiety, now you have double the trouble, double the stress and double the amount of mess to clean up when you get home.

Should I Crate My Dog?

Crating, in some cases, can make situations worse, especially if you go out and buy a crate and expect it to cure the problem.

It may save your house from getting destroyed but in a lot of cases dogs with severe separation anxiety can toilet in their crate or make attempts to break out causing injury to themselves as we already discussed with a past case of mine earlier in the book.

I did get a crate for Lady, but I made sure to train her to it first. I spent a lot of time and patience building up a positive association to the crate to make it feel like a safe place for her and eventually she learned to love it and chose to go there on her own accord as opposed to me having to force her into it as I see with a lot of clients when I go out and do assessments. If you have to force your dog into their crate, then trust me, they don't really like their crate, and they certainly have not built up a positive association with it.

Should I Hire a Dog Walker or Send My Dog to a Doggy Daycare?

I have mentioned more than once within this book that the RSPCA recommend leaving your dog alone for no longer than 4 hours at any one time.

You know how long you work. You know how long your dog is home alone for each day; therefore, only you can make that decision.

Personally, I would not feel comfortable leaving my dog for excess amounts of times. I think COVID-19 taught us one thing… it's actually really boring being stuck indoors for the majority of the day and trust me it is boring for your dog too.

Let us start by looking at the pros and cons of hiring a dog walker

By hiring a dog walker to come and walk your dog during the day, you help break up the day for your dog. You give your dog the chance to release some energy. You give your dog the chance to make use of his/her natural senses, therefore, providing mental stimulation as well.

It is an easy way to help break up the day for your dog; however, if you have not corrected your dog's separation anxiety and your dog walker is coming in to find wee and poop everywhere it is going to make their job more difficult and the time they spend having to clean up your dog's mess will reduce the amount of time your dog gets to go out for his/her walk.

Another potential issue and trust me I am certainly not discrediting the amazing work dog walkers do, but if they have had no experience with working with dogs suffering from separation anxiety, there is a good chance they could very easily and very quickly undo all of the hard work you have done so you may need to instruct them of the dos and the don'ts when you meet them to prevent any potential issues arising.

Let us move on by looking at the pros and cons of putting your dog into a doggy daycare

Doggy daycare centres are popping up here, there and everywhere, so how do you know which is the best one to choose?

Some daycare centres are literally a place where you drop off your dog, and they spend the whole day jumping and bounding around playing with their mates. Some would think that is great but guess what, it's not an ideal situation for your dog to be in.

As we have already mentioned dogs need structure and routine and as I do not have much experience with other daycare centres, let me tell you how the Pets2impress daycare centre runs which will hopefully help you when looking for the right daycare for you and your dog.

Help! My Dog Doesn't Like Being Left Alone

All of our dogs follow a day to day routine, so, for example, they all get 1-1 training sessions and group training sessions to help work on distractions. All of the dogs get involved in brain and scent games twice a day, they all go for two short walks, they get top to tail examinations, calms and cuddles, controlled play and most importantly they go down for naps. Do you remember earlier on in the book we discussed the importance of quiet times as part of your dog's day to day routine, well that is exactly why our dogs go down for naps.

A lot of our dogs also go out for Adventure days where we visit different locations on a 1-1 basis, working with the dog's lead training, recall training, undergo natural agility, playtime and scent work.

We also have a lot of our dogs that visit The Scent Space, which is a brand-new service we launched in June 2020. This is a room filled with different smells and textures to really encourage the dogs to make use of their natural senses. Think of it like a sensory room for children, but only this one is for dogs.

We have also recently introduced School trips where we take a number of dogs together to an enclosed field to work on their recall with distractions, undergo agility and create scent trails. The best part being that these dogs all get their own pack lunch to take along with them.

All of the daycare packages have a number of benefits to the dogs and to the owners, but most importantly each package ensures the dog's day follows a routine and is structured, keeping the dog happy and stimulated.

All daycare centres need to be legally licensed by the local authority, so this is certainly something you need to be asking when enquiring.

I think the one main benefit for enrolling your dog into a daycare centre is it gives them some time away from you in a positive environment. So whilst you are at work all day, you know that your dog is enjoying themselves, as opposed to being stressed at home alone.

Naturally, hiring a dog walker or enrolling your dog into a daycare is not going to help correct your dog's separation anxiety, that is something you need to do because there are always going to be times where you may need to leave your dog alone, it is not fair for the dog to have to be stressed and anxious when alone and by now I am sure you will agree there is a lot you can do to correct that.

Picking the right dog walker or daycare is a difficult task, and it is certainly similar to choosing the correct nursery for your children.

My youngest two go to private nursery two days a week, and I remember how long it took for us to find the one we thought would be perfect for us. We needed to make sure the opening times would suit our lifestyle, but most importantly, we wanted to check what others had to say about the nursery, so we read review after review. We then went and visited the nursery to get a feel for it and to meet the staff.

It's a worrying time leaving your child for the first time with people you do not know which is why we spent so long looking for the right one for us. It's a worrying time trusting someone you do not know with your dog, and that is why I strongly advise doing your homework first and taking the time to meet the staff, visiting the centre and getting a feel for the place.

I am a great believer in the fact if you do not get a positive feeling, then go with your gut and look elsewhere.

Reviews are there for a reason, make sure you look and hopefully you will find the right daycare for you and your dog.

Of course, daycare centres are not for every dog, some dogs love it, and others find it a difficult place to settle so any respectful daycare should offer assessments and trial days to make sure it will be the best option for your dog.

So within this chapter, we discussed a lot of mistakes many owners make and we looked at what you can do to ensure your dog is not left alone for long periods of times and I am sure you will agree there are many things you can do to prevent that. Sometimes it is just as simple as relying on the help of friends and family to check on your dog, but regardless, we must follow the RSPCA guidelines and not be leaving our dogs for any longer than 4 hours at any one time.

Chapter Ten

Your goal to success

Now that you have received all of the information you need to move forward with your dog, it is now time to start taking action.

You need to look at ways of reducing your dog's anxiety by following the advice given within this book. That may involve supplementing your dog with herbal remedies or looking at a potential diet change. Please remember these methods are not designed to change your dog's behaviour but more to give a helping hand to help reduce your dog's anxiety whilst you implement your new training plan and work on building up those gradual departure times.

Remember nothing in life is free and if you want to get the best from your dog, you need to implement this new programme to help build up confidence and independence and in turn reduce your dog's anxiety. This must be implemented by everyone within the household. Unfortunately, that may mean actually communicating with your family (I appreciate I am asking a lot) and working together. Things don't happen overnight and mistakes do happen but the more you communicate and the more you work together, the more you will achieve and you never know, you may actually realise that you like each other after all.

You need to establish a routine for your dog and stick to it, not just for this training programme but forevermore. You need to have set training times, set brain games, set playtimes, and again this involves everyone, not just Mam or Dad.

Start as you mean to go on. If you want your dog to be able to cope being left alone, then you must implement these changes; otherwise, why have you wasted your time reading this book?

Putting the above into action does not need to take forever, but once the above is in place, you are now ready to move forward with your new training plan.

Start with teaching your dog to settle, then identify and change your dog's association with those triggers then look at building up those gradual departure times. I cannot stress enough; at this stage, you must take your time, be patient and be consistent.

This process can be achieved in 1 week, four weeks sometimes even one year. We are all different, and we all learn at different paces; dogs are exactly the same so do not rush your dog and do not force him into a position where he feels uncomfortable or feels the need to have to react.

If you take your TIME (there is that word again), you are already on the road to success. Teaching your dog not to be afraid and to cope being left alone might take time, as it involves emotions. It may be the most time-consuming training that you have to do, but it is safe and sure. The best results are achieved if you do it carefully, step by step and focus on one thing at a time.

Understand that it is natural for a dog to be afraid, just like it is for us (you should see me watching a horror movie). Dogs cannot help it, and they are not reacting this way on purpose. It is up to us and your responsibility as a dog owner to help your dog overcome it.

If you follow the step by step guide issued within this book, it won't be long before you are able to leave your dog at home alone, knowing that he is able to cope. Just remember once again… we do not leave them for longer than 4 hours at any one time.

This is something I do with my dog on every walk and something we do with our daycare dogs. Wherever we go, we have an adventure, and we make use of the natural environment. For example, I often get Buddy jumping over falling down logs, weaving in and out of bollards, crawling underneath benches, balancing on walls, 1-1 training and scent work. It helps keep walks fun for Buddy and me.

As with us, sometimes we can take two steps forward and then feel we are taking four steps back, and this may happen from time to time with your dog during his training however do not be afraid to start again, remember the old saying 'Rome was not built in one day'… I don't actually know how long it took to build, but it certainly wasn't one day, and it certainly won't take one day to train your dog… trust me on that one.

Help! My Dog Doesn't Like Being Left Alone

Remember when following this guide to have fun, keep it light, and no matter what, do not give up. You have it in you to do it; you just need to believe that you can and you will.

One thing which I now swear by is a doggy cam, and I would certainly advise (if you have not already got one) to purchase one. With this, you can check in on your dog to make sure he is coping and if not, then the answer is simple, go back a step and practice some more.

I do feel as the book has come to an end that now is the time to say this one final time, to get the results you want, you must take your time, be patient and be consistent.

Bonuses

I hope you have enjoyed reading this book, and I hope it has left you feeling motivated and ready to tackle this issue. Just remember that this book is only valuable if you take action.

I do appreciate that there is only so much you can take away from a book which is why I have decided to share some free gifts with you.

My first gift to you is a free copy of the Pets2impress Training guide.

Click on the link below to grab your copy

https://mailchi.mp/17e466208370/free-training-guide

My second gift to you is free access to our online Pawfect Pooch tutorial videos to demonstrate some basic training techniques discussed within this book that you can start with your dog to help keep them focused and mentally stimulated.

To access these videos, please visit the following links:

The Pawfect Pooch – Tutorial videos	
Introduction	https://youtu.be/aF2kNx5A3QY
Teaching your dog his name	https://youtu.be/Svod7ZSQ3ag
Toilet Training	https://youtu.be/Qq0T3Jfve8A
Play Biting	https://youtu.be/BUnbCqNOhZQ

Help! My Dog Doesn't Like Being Left Alone

Helping your dog cope being left alone	https://youtu.be/9iECfeUMwiU
Sit/Stand/Down	https://youtu.be/FqxDO5izQ9g
Sit/Stay	https://youtu.be/p63FviEq1r8
Lead Training videos 1-4	https://youtu.be/0k7oT-gkkAs https://youtu.be/zS50qzonGKI https://youtu.be/rNr4kYmjE_A https://youtu.be/cMgWKw3Xkdo
The Watch command	https://youtu.be/mtya0Jb25cU
Recall	https://youtu.be/Ui6AOE0-fvg
Jumping up	https://youtu.be/yjEjUrlg1GQ
Leave it command	https://youtu.be/a1mHq4cyS0Q
The bed command	https://youtu.be/WUMUbpLrliU
Health Checks	https://youtu.be/HqN3rXAQg6M
Tricks	https://youtu.be/S2sjM3P_Dhw
Canine First Aid	https://youtu.be/qTpVeyLcoog

My third gift to you is free access to our private Facebook page. This was originally set up for those that signed up to the online Pawfect Pooch course. You can showcase your progress along the way and get instant access to me if you have any questions.

To access the private Facebook page, please visit the following link:

https://www.facebook.com/groups/852341085262009/

The value of these tutorials and training guide is worth £100, so don't say I never give you anything. I hope you find them of use.

About the Author

Tim Jackson started his career working with animals as a veterinary auxiliary nurse. He trained and qualified as a veterinary nurse in 2007 at Myerscough College. He was promoted to Head veterinary nurse and spent a number of years helping animals and their owners.

In 2008, Tim launched Pets2impress, a company that took the region by storm. What began as a pet sitting service soon expanded to offer a variety of services.

In 2013, Tim took the decision to leave his position as Head Veterinary nurse to expand Pets2impress.

Tim has completed multiple animal behaviour courses, including the Think Dog Certificates and a Diploma in Animal Behaviour. He passed each of these with a distinction and the knowledge he gained from these, combined with his extensive nursing experience, allowed him to offer one-on-one training sessions for all problem behaviours utilising only positive, reward-based training programmes.

This is a fun and stress-free method of training, which is easy to learn and rapidly achieves fantastic results. In its most basic form, it is a method of communication that is very clear for the dog. Examples of problem behaviours which Tim is able to assist with include separation anxiety, lack of basic training, dog-on-dog aggression and other anxiety-related issues, however, no problem is too small or too big for Tim.

In 2015, Tim opened a state of the art daycare facility, offering a safe and stimulating environment for dogs whilst their owners' are out at work. His experience as a qualified veterinary nurse, dog trainer and canine behaviourist gave him a comprehensive understanding that all dogs have different physical and emotional needs, allowing daycare sessions to be tailor-made to suit each individual.

Tim runs his daycare as close to a nursery setting as possible and therefore follows a daily schedule as closely as possible. This is extremely beneficial to the dogs in his care as it has been well documented that dogs thrive off predictability, and it has positive effects on both their behaviour and mental wellbeing.

A typical day at the daycare centre includes free play, walks outside for a change of scenery, training-time, and quiet time as rest is extremely important to prevent overstimulation, which can have a negative impact on both behaviour and physical condition. In October 2019, Tim launched an additional package to the daycare service, the doggy 'adventure' daycare to offer dog's further opportunity to receive physical and mental stimulation on a 1-1 basis as well as receive the other benefits daycare has to offer. In June 2020, Tim launched two additional packages to the daycare service, The Scent Space and School Trips as with the adventure daycares these were designed to allow dogs further opportunity to receive physical and mental stimulation.

Tim is well known for his sense of humour and love and dedication to the welfare of all animals. Tim has owned several animals over the years including a rescue tarantula (which he was absolutely terrified of), an iguana, bearded dragons, cats, hamsters, rats, mice, fish and dogs.

Tim's mission in life is to help owners who struggle with their dog to prevent dogs ending up in shelter.

When not working Tim can be seen swapping Doggy daycare for Daddy daycare. Tim loves nothing more than spending time with his three adorable children. He can also be found out walking his dog Buddy and every now and then enjoys a nice pint at the local pub.

To find out more about Tim and Pets2impress please visit the Pets2impress website www.pets2impress.com

Other Books by the Author

Available to purchase from www.pets2impress.com and Amazon

Dog Training Book

Help! My dog is a devil with other dogs

Acknowledgements

As this is my second book, there are so many people I would like to thank, so many people that have supported me over the years and pushed me to always try harder. I definitely forgot to say thanks to certain people in my last book, oops… I'll try harder in this book.

My first thanks must go to my adorable dog, Lady. Had Lady not developed separation anxiety, I would never have found my passion for canine behaviour and training. She brought me 12 years of love, loyalty and support. There is not a day goes by where I do not think about her or miss her. Gone, but certainly not forgotten. Those that have visited the Pets2impress Daycare centre will have seen that her memory still lives on and always will.

To my family and friends, who are always there when I need them. I wouldn't be the person I am today without you.

Special thanks to my wife, Rebecca, and my three adorable children, Sienna, Harvey and Darcey. They give me a purpose to continue working hard.

Special thanks to my good friends Tim Strange and Annouska Muzyczuk who have always stuck by me through thick and thin.

To my mentor, Dominic Hodgson, for his guidance and support and for continuing to push me forward.

To my good friend, Katie Gee from Dogwood Adventure Play, for recommending me to Dominic Hodgson and for your support over the years. Working together at Dogs Trust, she tolerated a lot of shit from me as we travelled around the country.

To my good friend, Shannon, who is always a phone call away should I ever need to talk or in some cases moan.

To my good friend Georgie, who is my training partner and who encourages me to keep going even when I really do not want to.

To my good friend, Suresh, who has always encouraged and guided me and has always helped me out when I needed him.

To the staff at Pets2impress, Shannon, Lauren, Abby, Abbey, Terri and Karen 1. For putting up with me all of these years and laughing at my not so funny jokes and 2. For your support, enthusiasm and shared love you have for the dogs in our care. I couldn't do the job I do without my amazing team.

To my Pets2impress clients, who have been loyal to Pets2impress all these years. I would not be where I am today without your support, recommendations and dedication.

To the veterinary staff, who I used to work with for their support and recommendations over the years. They certainly had to put up with a lot from me, from singing constantly to winding each of them up on a daily basis. I certainly miss working with them every day.

My final thanks must go to you. Thank you for choosing this book and spending the time to read it. I hope you found it useful and I hope you start to action the points made in this book. My mission is to try and prevent as many dogs ending up in shelter if possible, and if this book helps others, then I can sleep well at night. I ask if you found this book useful that you leave a review on Amazon… I will accept no less than a 5-star rating.

Tim Jackson, RVNBCCSDip.Fda

Printed in Great Britain
by Amazon